How to use

  1 Find a time and place when you can read the Bible each day.

 **2** Get your Bible, a pencil and your XTB notes.

3 Ask God to help you to understand what you read.

 **4** Read today's XTB page and Bible bit.

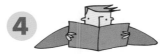 **5** Pray about what you have read and learnt.

  **6** If you can, talk to an adult or a friend about what you've learnt.

This copy of XTB comes with a free **Bible Mini Map Book**.

We'll use it to explore three Bible books—Exodus, Matthew and Acts.

These Bible books are full of exciting (and dangerous!) journeys. You can follow them in the map book.

Are you ready to try out your MINI MAP BOOK? Then hurry on to Day 1.

DAY 1 FAR TREK

Follow the footprints into the Book of Acts.

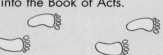

Acts tells us about Paul's three missionary journeys. What's a missionary?—a man with a mission...

Mission Impossible? No! Paul's mission is to tell loads of people about **Jesus**. It will be dangerous—but the Holy Spirit will help him.

Walk and Talk Everywhere Paul walked, he also talked about Jesus.

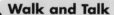

We're going to stride out with Paul on his **second** missionary journey.

Sneak a Peek Check out page 1 of the **XTB Mini Map Book** to see where Paul went on his journeys.

Sail Away Sometimes Paul even sailed to other countries, so he could tell people there about Jesus too.

No Rambling Here! Paul made his message very clear. He told people that the <u>only</u> way to be right with God is to put your trust in **Jesus**.

But there's a problem. Jog along to the next page to find out what it was...

Welcome to xtb Issue Three

Comings and Goings

xtb

XTB stands for **eXplore The Bible**.

Read a bit of the Bible each day.
Escape from Egypt with the thrilling book of **Exodus**.
Zoom in on **Matthew** to investigate Jesus' teaching and miracles.
Join Paul on a dangerous journey in the book of **Acts**.

Are you ready to explore the Bible? Fill in the bookmark...
...then turn over the page to start exploring with XTB!

Table Talk FOR FAMILIES

Look out for **Table Talk** — a book to help children and adults explore the Bible together. It can be used by:

- Families
- One adult with one child
- Children's leaders with their groups
- Any other way you want to try

Table Talk uses the same Bible passages as XTB so that they can be used together if wanted. You can buy Table Talk from your local Good Book Company website:
UK: www.thegoodbook.co.uk • North America: www.thegoodbook.com
Australia: www.thegoodbook.com.au • New Zealand: www.thegoodbook.co.nz

xtb

This book belongs to
.......Mimi.........................

Sometimes I'm called
.......Madeleine....... (nickname)

My birthday is
.....11th of June.................

My age is
........7.............................

My favourite dinosaur is
......T-rex.........................

How to find your way around the Bible...

**Look out for the READ sign.
It tells you what Bible bit to read.**

**READ
Acts 15v1-5**

**So, if the notes say... READ Acts 15v1-5
...this means chapter 15 and verses 1 to 5
...and this is how you find it.**

Use the **Contents** page in your Bible to find where Acts begins

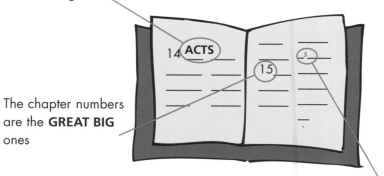

The chapter numbers are the **GREAT BIG** ones

The verse numbers are the tiny ones!

**Oops! Keep getting lost?
Cut out this bookmark and use it to keep your place.**

ADDING UP

Paul told people the fantastic message about Jesus. But he heard that some people were **adding** stuff to the message…

READ
Acts 15v1-5

Spot six differences between these two pictures.

Some people were saying that to be right with God you needed to keep Jewish rules <u>as well as</u> trusting in Jesus. Paul knew this was very wrong!

Did you know?

Circumcision meant having a small piece of skin cut off. It was a sign of being part of God's family. These people were saying that you had to be circumcised as well as trusting in Jesus.

Acts
15v1-5

Where did Paul and Barnabas go? (v2)

J eresalam

Paul went to see the Christian leaders in Jerusalem for a big meeting. They had to decide whether Christians had to keep the Jewish law or not. It was a very important decision to make.
(We'll find out what they decided tomorrow…)

As Paul and Barnabas travelled to Jerusalem they told everyone they met how loads of Gentiles (non-Jews) had become followers of Jesus (v3). Everyone was very excited.

THINK + PRAY

Are **you** excited when you hear about people following Jesus? Thank God that every day more and more people around the world become followers of Jesus.

RED LETTER DAY

You need to trust in Jesus.

Paul

You need to trust in Jesus **and** obey the Jewish law.

Some others

Who was right? That was the important question that the Christian leaders had to answer. It was a l-o-n-g meeting. *Fill in the tops of each letter to pick out **two key points**.*

Peter

It is through the grace of our **LORD JESUS** that we are saved. (v11)

This is the <u>most important point</u>. The <u>only</u> way to be right with God is by believing in **Jesus**. Don't believe anyone who tells you that you have to do other stuff as well (*like going to a particular church, or praying in a special way*). **You don't!!**

We should not make it **DIFFICULT** for the Gentiles who are turning to God. (v19)

James

The Gentiles (non-Jews) were put right with God by **believing in Jesus**. They didn't have to keep the Jewish law. But James didn't want to make things difficult for the Jewish believers either. So he told the Gentiles to avoid doing things that would offend the Jewish Christians.

It was decided to send two of the leaders from Jerusalem back with Paul and Barnabas. They took a letter with them.

READ
Acts 15v30-35

Copy all the **red letters** (in order) to see what the letter was designed to do.

encourage

The letter was *encouraging*. Judas and Silas were *encouraging* too. They wanted to encourage the new Christians to keep following Jesus.

THINK + PRAY

Sometimes, we do things that make it harder for our friends to become Christians. (For example, if we are unkind or ignore them, they may think that Christians don't care about others.)

Ask God to help you to tell your friends about Jesus, and not to do anything that might put them off turning to Him.

DAY 3 WHAT A BARNY

It was time for Paul to set off on his **second missionary journey**. His mission?—to see how the new Christians were getting on, and to tell more people about Jesus. But there was a problem...

READ
Acts 15v36-41

Who did Barnabas want to take? (v37) _John, mark_

Did you know?

John Mark was Barnabas' cousin. He was sometimes called John and sometimes Mark! He was the same guy who wrote the book of Mark (*Mark's Gospel*) in the Bible.

John Mark had travelled with Paul and Barnabas before, but he had given up part way. So Paul didn't want to take him again.

Paul and Barnabas had a big argument about it.
They decided to split up.

 xtb Acts 15v36-41

Fill in the gaps.

Barnabas and **M**_ark_ went from **Antioch** to **C**_yprus_ . (v39)

Paul and **S**_ilas_ went from **Antioch**, through **C**_ilicicia_ to **Derbe** and **Lystra**. (v 40-41 & 16v1)

Find the map on page 2 of your **Mini Map Book**. Draw in **Barnabas'** journey with a **dotted line**. Draw in **Paul's** journey with a **solid line**.

 What a sad story. Paul and Barnabas had such a bad argument that they had to split up. *But look again at the lines on your map.* Now there were <u>two</u> journeys, and <u>two</u> places that would hear about Jesus. God took this **sad** event, and brought **good** out of it!

PRAY Ask God to help you not to spoil your friendships with arguments. Ask Him to help you to say sorry and put things right if you do.

A PUZZLING CHOICE

Acts 16v1-5

Paul and Silas had reached the town of Lystra. *Follow the lines to see who they met there.*

Thomas

Titus

Timothy

Tabitha

Paul wanted to take Timothy on the journey with them, but he decided to do something very puzzling first...

READ
Acts 16v1-5

Fill in the family tree from verse 1.

His dad was a
G reek

His mum was a
J ewish

T imothey

Jewish boys were circumcised (a small piece of skin cut off) when they were 8 days old. But although Timothy's mum was Jewish, his dad wasn't, and Timothy <u>hadn't</u> been circumcised.

Did **Paul** circumcise Timothy? (v3) **Yes / No**

THINK SPOT Do you remember the argument on Day1? Some people thought you had to be circumcised to be a Christian. Paul knew that was **wrong**. He <u>didn't</u> circumcise Timothy to make him a Christian. Timothy was <u>already</u> a Christian. Paul did it so that <u>other Jews</u> might accept Timothy, and listen to what he told them about Jesus.

Did you find that hard to understand? If so, ask an older Christian to help you.

THINK + PRAY Sometimes we need **help** to understand the Bible, and to keep following Jesus. That's what Paul, Silas and Timothy did as they went from town to town. Who helps <u>you</u> to learn from the Bible and to keep following Jesus?

_____

Thank God for them.

PAUL & CO—WHERE TO GO?

 Acts 16v6-10

Paul, Silas and Timothy carried on with the second missionary journey. But how were they to decide where to go?

First, God told them **where <u>not</u> to go!** *Take the first letter of each picture to work out the place names.*

a s i a

b i t h d n i a

Then God told them **where to go.**

m a c e d o n i a

Look out for these places as you read the Bible verses.

READ
Acts 16v6-10

Twice, the Holy Spirit <u>stopped</u> Paul from going somewhere! Then, during the night, Paul had a vision—a dream sent by God. He saw a man from Macedonia (Northern Greece).

What did the man in Paul's dream say? (v9)

Come over and help us!

On his first journey, Paul had not gone as far as Greece, but this time God wanted him to go further.

This was the first time that the good news about Jesus had reached **Europe.**

THINK + PRAY

Do you live in Europe? _____

Wherever you live, thank God that the great news about Jesus has reached you too.

Yesterday we saw how God showed Paul and Co. where to go. Draw their route on page 3 of your **Mini Map Book**.

Draw a line ‿‿‿ from **Lystra** to **Troas** to **Samothrace** to **Neapolis** to **Philippi**.

Who did Paul see in yesterday's dream? (v9)

A **man** from M_____

But when Paul reached Philippi (in Macedonia) he actually met up with some women!

READ
Acts 16v11-15

Circle the correct words.

Paul and Co. went to the **church / school / river** to find a place of **peace / prayer / potatoes**. They spoke to the **men / women / children** who were there. One of them was called **Lydia / Lynne / Linda**. She sold **purple / pink / peach** cloth. God opened her **heart / mind** to the great news about Jesus. She became a believer and was baptised. Then she invited Paul and Co. to her **wedding / party / house**.

Wow! Lydia had become a believer. She persuaded Paul and the others to stay at her house. It probably became the meeting place for the Christians in Philippi.

THINK + PRAY

As soon as she became a believer, Lydia wanted to **help** Paul. Do you know anyone who tells other people about Jesus? How could you **help** them? (Could you send them a letter or email to tell them that you are praying for them? Could you give some money to help support their work? *If you're not sure who you could help, or how to help them, ask an older Christian or someone at your church.*) Think carefully about what you want to do to help this person. Now ask God to help you to do it.

DAY 7 GO TO JAIL!

In Philippi, Paul and Silas met a suffering slave-girl.

READ
Acts 16v16-18

The slave-girl was being controlled by an evil spirit. This meant that she could tell the future. Her owners made a lot of money from her fortune telling.

What did she say about Paul and Silas? (v17)

> They are **s**_____ of the Most High **G**_____. They are telling you how to be **s**_____.

She was right —but Paul was worried.

This slave-girl was involved in **evil** stuff, and Paul didn't want people to connect **Jesus** with those things. So Paul told the spirit it had to leave her.

Did the spirit leave the slave-girl? (v18) **Yes / No**

Did you know?

Paul was able to free the girl from the evil spirit, through **Jesus' power**. Jesus is the Most High God—and <u>nobody</u> is more powerful than Him!

The owners of the slave-girl couldn't make money out of her any more. They were furious! So they told lies about Paul and Silas to get them into trouble with the Romans...

READ
Acts 16v22-24

Paul and Silas were beaten and thrown into prison, with their feet locked into the stocks. *Draw the stocks round their feet.*

It looked hopeless. But it wasn't! As we'll see tomorrow, **God** was in control...

PRAY

Even in prison, Paul and Silas knew that nobody was more powerful than God. As we'll see tomorrow, they kept on trusting Him.

Ask God to help <u>you</u> to trust Him, even when things are hard.

DAY 8 GET OUT OF JAIL FREE

Paul and Silas had been beaten, thrown into jail and chained up. How do you think they felt? *Draw their faces.*

Now check what Acts says. **READ** Acts 16v25

Paul and Silas were singing!! *Draw their faces again!*

Think Hard
How would <u>you</u> answer the jailer's question?

Now look at **Paul's** answer.

READ Acts 16v29-34

Paul told the jailer all about J̲e̲s̲u̲s̲

The jailer and his whole family became followers of Jesus. Now they were **full of joy.**

Suddenly, the jail was shaken by an... EARTHQUAKE!	The doors flew open... ...and the chains fell off.	The jailer woke up. Oh No! The prisoners have escaped!

I will be killed for this. I may as well die now	But Paul stopped him. Don't harm yourself. We're all here!	The jailer was amazed! He had an important question. What must I do to be saved?

PRAY Are you a follower of Jesus? Does that make you full of joy too? If it does, tell Jesus about it!

Use the Arrow Code to find out what Paul was teaching.

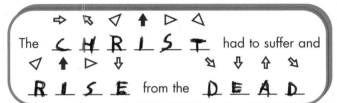

The **C H R I S T** had to suffer and **R I S E** from the **D E A D**

J E S U S is the Christ.

Arrow Code

A= ⇧
C= ⇨
D= ⬂
E= ⇩
H= ⬃
I= ⬆
J= ⬀
R= ◁
S= ▷
T= ◁
U= ▽

Did you know?

Christ is a Greek word. **Messiah** is Hebrew. They both mean 'God's Chosen King'. God had promised to send a King to rescue His people. Paul was teaching that **Jesus** is this King.

Yesterday, Paul and Silas were in prison in Philippi. Read the verses to find out where they moved on to when they were released.

READ
Acts 17v1-4

Find page 3 in your **Mini Map Book**.
Draw a line from Philippi to Thessalonica.

Many people in Thessalonica believed Paul's message and became followers of Jesus. But some people were jealous. They got an angry mob together and started a riot! So Paul and Silas had to escape.

READ **Acts 17v10** to see where they went.

Paul and Silas escaped to **Berea**.
Draw a line from Thessalonica to Berea on your map.

Paul told the people in Thessalonica that Jesus **had to die** and come back to life. In a few days, Paul will be explaining <u>why</u> to people in Athens.

PRAY **Dear God, thank you for sending Jesus as our King, just as You promised to do.**

a MaN

DAY 10 CHECK IT OUT!

Match each word and picture.
One is done for you.

Checkmate

Chequered Flag

Check-Up

Checkpoint

Checkout

What's all this 'checking' about?
Check it out in today's Bible verses!

READ
Acts 17v10-15

Did you spot what the Bereans did?
They **checked** Paul out! What did
they **check** with? (v11)

The S*criptures*

Did you know?

The 'Scriptures' are the Old Testament
part of the Bible. The Bereans were
checking that what Paul said really did
come from the Bible.

Having checked what
Paul said, many Bereans
believed in Jesus. But then some of
Paul's enemies from Thessalonica
found out that he was in Berea. They
made so much trouble for Paul that he
had to leave. He went to Athens
instead. *More about that tomorrow...*

THINK SPOT

When you do your **XTB**
page, are you ever tempted
to skip the Bible reading and
just do the puzzles?
Please don't! It's really
important that you read the
Bible for yourself, and **check**
that what I've written really is true!

*Do the same at church. If you are not
sure about something you are taught,
ask where it comes in the Bible. Then
check it out for yourself.*

PRAY

Thank God for the
Bible—which teaches
you all you need to
know about Jesus.
Ask God to help you
to understand the Bible
as you read it.

DAY 11 IDOL TALK

1 WHAT PAUL SAW

Finish this picture of the Parthenon.

Athens is the capital of Greece. It is full of ancient buildings (like the Parthenon), and beautiful statues.

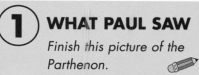

When Paul visited Athens 2000 years ago, the city was famous. People came from far and wide to visit it.

2 WHAT PAUL FELT

But Paul <u>wasn't</u> delighted by the beauty he saw. He felt something very different...

READ
Acts 17v16-17

How did Paul feel? (v16)

TROUBLED

He was upset because the buildings and statues in Athens were made in praise of <u>pretend</u> gods (idols).

PAUL IN ATHENS

3 WHAT PAUL DID

Paul told people about Jesus. (v17)

Fill in the missing vowels (aeiou).

He went to the **SYN****V****G**o**G**u**Q** (v17) (*where Jewish people met to pray and learn from the Old Testament*).

He went to the **M**a**RK**o**T—PL**a**C**o (v17) (*where he talked with anyone who happened to be there*).

He took every opportunity to tell people about Jesus.

4 WHAT PAUL SAID

He told them about **Jesus**. *We'll find out exactly what he said tomorrow.*

Like the people in Athens, most people today know very little about Jesus. They are more interested in money, sport, pop music or clothes. These matter more to them than God.

PRAY Do any of your friends think these things are more important than God? How does this make you feel? Talk to God about it.

DAY 12 WHAT'S GOD LIKE?

Some of the people Paul met in Athens wanted to hear more. They took him to the Areopagus—the city council.

READ
Acts 17v19-23

While walking round Athens, Paul had seen many altars (where people gave gifts to their gods). What did one of them say on it? (v23)

TO AN Unknown **GOD**

Paul told the people all about this God they didn't know.

Crack the code to see three of the things Paul said about God.

A=◗ D=▢ E=■ G=○ J=●
L=▲ M=▼ R=◆ S=❖ U=◉

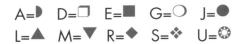

God _M A D E_ the world, and everything in it.

God _R U L E S_ the world. He's in charge.

God will _J U D G E_ the world, and everyone in it.

The first part of Paul's speech told the people of Athens that **God** is completely different from idols. Their idols were just statues made by human hands. **But God isn't!!** God <u>made</u> and <u>rules</u> everything—including them!

Paul also told them that God would be their <u>Judge</u>. *More about that tomorrow.*

PRAY

Paul needed to tell the people in Athens about God because they didn't know Him. **We** can get to know God by reading **His Word** to us, the Bible. Ask God to help you to get to know Him better and better as you read the Bible.

JESUS THE JUDGE

Check out **yesterday's page** to see what Paul said about God...

1 God **Made** us.

2 God **Rules** over us.

3 God will **Judge** us.

Paul told the people of Athens that God made us all—so we are all His offspring (children). Then Paul went on to explain what we need to **do**, and **why**.

READ
Acts 17v29-34

Paul told the people that they had to **repent** (to turn from their wrong ways).

Add the missing vowels (aeiou) to find out why.

A d_a_y is c_o_ming wh_e_n w_e_ will _a_ll be J_u_dged by J_e_sus. (v31)

How could Paul's hearers (and us) be sure about this? (v31)

Because God raised Jesus from the d_e_a_d.

Did you know?

Raised • Risen • Resurrection
These words all mean a dead person coming back to life.

Some of the people listening to Paul just laughed at him. But others believed what he told them, and became followers of Jesus.

Turn over to **Judge and Rescuer** on the next page to find out more. ➡

Time to Think
- Are **you** a follower of Jesus?
- Do you want to be?
  (*Go back to **Judge and Rescuer** if you're not sure.*)
- Do you want to tell your friends about Jesus like Paul did?

PRAY **Talk to God about your answers. Ask Him to help you.**

JUDGE AND RESCUER

JESUS IS OUR JUDGE

Paul told the people in Athens that a day is coming when we will all be judged by Jesus. **But there's a problem!** We are all guilty—because we all sin.

What is Sin?

Sin is more than just doing wrong things. We all like to be in charge of our own lives. We do what **we** want instead of what **God** wants. This is called Sin.

Sin gets in the way between us and God. It stops us from knowing Him and stops us from being His friends.

Because we all sin, we are all guilty.

Write GUILTY under the picture. _____

JESUS IS OUR RESCUER

But the great news is that Jesus came to **rescue** us from our sins!

How did Jesus rescue us?

At the first Easter, when Jesus was about 33 years old, He was crucified. He was nailed to a cross and left to die.

As He died, all the sins of the world (all the wrongs people do) were put onto Jesus. He took all of our sin onto Himself, taking the punishment we deserve. He died in our place, as our Rescuer, so that we can be forgiven.

When Jesus died He dealt with the problem of sin. He was found **Guilty**, so that we can be found **Not Guilty**. That means that there is nothing to separate us from God any more. That's great news for you and me!

Write NOT GUILTY under the picture.

We can know God today as our Friend and King—and one day live in heaven with Him for ever.

> ### Did you know?
> Jesus died on the cross as our Rescuer—but He didn't stay dead! After three days God brought Him back to life! Jesus is still alive today, ruling as our King.

Have YOU been rescued by Jesus? Turn to the next to find out more

AM I A CHRISTIAN?

Not sure if you're a Christian? Then check it out below...

Christians are people who have been rescued by Jesus and follow Him as their King.

You can't become a Christian by trying to be good.

That's great news, since you can't be totally good all the time!

It's about accepting what Jesus did on the cross to rescue you. To do it, you will need to **ABCD**.

A **Admit** your sin—that you do, say and think wrong things. Tell God you are sorry. Ask Him to forgive you, and to help you to change. There will be some wrong things you have to stop doing.

B **Believe** that Jesus died for you, to take the punishment for your sin; that He came back to life, and that He is still alive today.

C **Consider** the cost of living like God's friend from now on, with Him in charge. It won't be easy. Ask God to help you do this.

D **Do** something about it! In the past you've gone your own way rather than God's way. Will you hand control of your life over to Him from now on? If you're ready to ABCD, then talk to God now. The prayer will help you.

A prayer

Dear God,
I have done and said and thought things that are wrong. I am really sorry. Please forgive me. Thank you for sending Jesus to die for me. From now on, please help me to live as one of Your friends, with You in charge.   Amen

Jesus welcomes <u>everyone</u> who comes to Him. If you have put your trust in Him, He has rescued you from your sins and will help you to live for Him. That's brilliant!

INTENT ON TEACHING

When Paul left Athens, he went to **Corinth**. Find the map on page 4 of your **Mini Map Book**. Draw a <u>statue</u> by Athens (to remind you of the *idols* they believed in). Now draw a <u>tent</u> near Corinth.

Can you guess why you've drawn a tent?

a) Paul stayed in a tent.

b) Paul made tents.

c) Paul joined a circus.

Read the Bible verses to find out.

READ
Acts 18v1-5

We're coming to the end of Paul's second missionary journey. All the time his **mission** has been to tell people about Jesus. But now we find him doing **another job** as well.

What was it? (v3)

Making tent makers

Did you know?

Paul could have asked the Christians in Corinth for money—but he didn't want to be a burden to them. Paul wrote about this later in his letter to them.
You can read it for yourself in 2 Corinthians 11v9.

Who joined Paul in Corinth? (v5)

Silos **and T**imothdthy

They brought gifts and money with them, which meant that Paul was able to stop tentmaking. Instead, he started teaching about Jesus every day.

PRAY

Pray for anyone you know who teaches other people about Jesus. (*Maybe in other countries, or at your church or school.*) Ask God to give them everything they need to be able to keep teaching about Jesus.

ha.er: b) Paul was a tentmaker.

DAY 15 JOURNEY'S END

xtb   Acts 18v5-11

We're coming to the end of Paul's second missionary **journey**. He's in Corinth, teaching **Jewish** people about Jesus. But some of the Jews became angry and tried to **stop** Paul—so he started teaching the **Gentiles** (non-Jews) instead. Many people **believed** what Paul was teaching them, and became followers of Jesus.

Then one night Paul had a dream. *Fit the underlined words into the puzzle to find out who Paul saw in his dream.*

Find out more about Paul's dream in the Bible verses...

READ
Acts 18v9-11

What did Jesus say to Paul? (v9)

Do not be afraid

Keep on talking

Jesus promised that no-one in Corinth would harm Paul. So Paul stayed for a long time, telling people about Jesus.

How long did Paul stay in Corinth? (v11)   year and a half

THINK + PRAY

All through Paul's journey he kept on telling people about Jesus. Even when things got tough, or people tried to stop him, he carried on speaking.
Who could you talk to about Jesus?
_____
You might find it hard to tell them about Jesus. Ask God to help you.

DAY 16 ESCAPE FROM EGYPT!

Read the Hieroglyphics to find out who needs to escape from Egypt.

i S R A e L i T e S

At the beginning of the book of Exodus, the Israelites are living in Ancient Egypt. But they are <u>not</u> Egyptians!

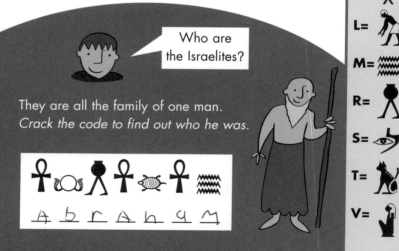

Who are the Israelites?

They are all the family of one man.
Crack the code to find out who he was.

A b R A h ? M

A= ☥
B= ◯◯
E= 𓅓
H= 𓆰
I= 𓎛
L= 𓀀
M= 〰〰〰
R= 𓀁
S= 👁
T= 🐈
V= 𓃠

God had made three amazing promises to Abraham:

1 LAND

2 CHILDREN

3 BLESSING

God promised to give Abraham's family the land of Canaan to live in.

God said that Abraham's family would be so HUGE that there would be too many to count!

God promised that someone from Abraham's family would be God's way of blessing the whole world.

If God promised to give them **Canaan** to live in, why are they in **Egypt**?

Years after Abraham had died, there was a terrible famine in Canaan. The food ran out. If the family stayed in Canaan they would all die.

But God used **Joseph** (who was Abraham's great grandson) to save the whole family. They moved to Egypt, where there was plenty of food for them to eat.

More on the next page.

DAY 16 OODLES OF ISRAELITES

CONTINUED

xtb Exodus 1v1-11

Find page 5 of your **Mini Map Book**.
*Draw the journey the Israelites made
from **Canaan** to **Egypt**.*

Did you know?

You can read the story of Joseph in
chapters 37 to 50 of the book of
Genesis.

READ
Exodus 1v8-11

The new Pharaoh
(king of Egypt)
was worried. He
thought the
Israelites were dangerous.

He was scared that
they would help
Egypt's enemies. So
he turned them into... ➡️ S L A V E S

Pharaoh wanted to keep the Israelites as his slaves.
But **God** had promised that they would live in the land of
Canaan. The scene was now set for a big showdown between
God and Pharaoh. *No prizes for guessing who wins!!*

The Israelites stayed in Egypt for **400 years!**
By then there were **oodles** of them...

READ
Exodus 1v6-7

Had God kept His promise to give
Abraham a huge family? (v7)   **Yes / No**

This family is H–U–G–E. But they also have a huge problem...

PRAY

Exodus is a great book to read if you
want to find out what God is really like.
**Ask God to help you to get to know
Him better and better as you read
through Exodus.**

DAY 17 HAPPY BIRTH DAY?

Pharaoh had turned the Israelites into **slaves**. He forced them to do back-breaking **work**, building cities and working in the fields. They were treated really **badly** by their slave masters. But they carried on having more and more **children**—and the number of Israelites grew and **grew**.

Find all the underlined words in the wordsearch. Some are backwards!

Then Pharaoh came up with a terrible plan...

READ
Exodus 1v15-17

The midwives helped the Israelite women to give birth. Pharaoh told the midwives to <u>kill</u> any baby boys who were born! They were only to let the <u>girls</u> live.

Did the midwives do what Pharaoh commanded? (v17) no

There is a very important question that runs through the book of Exodus. You can find it on the **bottom row** of the wordsearch. (*It's written backwards!*) Copy it here.

W<u>ho is the King</u>?

THINK SPOT

Because Pharaoh was the king of Egypt, he thought that <u>he</u> was the most important person around. But the midwives knew the <u>real</u> answer to the question. They knew that **God** is the real King. He's the **King of Kings**. So they did what God wanted, instead of what Pharaoh had said.

PRAY

Dear God, thank you that You are the real King of our world. Thank you that no-one and nothing can stop Your plans from working out. *Amen*

xtb Exodus 1v22 - 2v10

What was yesterday's important question?

Wh○ ⅰs th℮ K⎸ng ?

Today's story shows the answer very clearly. But first we find out about Pharaoh's next horrible plan...

READ
Exodus 1v22

Pharaoh tried to use the river Nile to _destroy_ the Israelites.

But instead, **God** was going to use the river to _save_ them!!

READ
Exodus 2v1-10

Copy the pictures into the gaps.

An Israelite couple had a baby boy. They hid him for **3** months. Then his mum put him carefully into a She put the basket among some reeds on the bank of the river Nile. The baby's sister to see what would happen. After a while, Pharaoh's daughter came down to the She saw the basket, and sent her slave girl to get it. When she saw the baby, he was The baby's sister offered to find an Israelite to look after the baby. She brought his own mum! Later, when the boy was older, he went to live with Pharaoh's daughter. She called him **Moses**

Wow! God used the river to _save_ Moses. Later, He would use Moses to _save_ the Israelites!

PRAY **Thank God that He's in control and that His plans always work out.**

WHO CHOSE YOU?

Exodus 2v11-15

Crack the Hieroglyphics code.

Who made you our R U L e R

and I e D G e ?

Look out for this question as you read the passage.

READ
Exodus 2v11-15

Circle the correct words.

Moses saw an Egyptian **beating/heating/cheating** an Israelite slave. Moses **filled/drilled/killed** the Egyptian, and buried him in the **band/stand/sand**. The next day, Moses saw two Israelites **fighting/lighting/writing**. When he tried to stop them, they asked, "Who made you our ruler and **fudge/judge/nudge**?" When Pharaoh found out, he tried to kill Moses. So Moses **fled/shed/bread** to Midian.

C=
D=
E=
G=
J=
L=
O=
R=
S=
U=

The book of **Acts** tells us a bit more about this story. This is what it says:

"Moses thought his own people would realise that

God was using him to R e S C e ___ them. But they did not." *Acts 7v25*

If you already know the story of Moses, you will know that God had chosen Moses to rescue the Israelites. But it wasn't **the right time** yet. When it <u>was</u> the right time, God would bring Moses back to Egypt.

PRAY

The Israelites hadn't even asked God for help yet, but He <u>knew</u> that they needed to be rescued. Matthe 6v8 says 'Your Father already k' what you need before you ask Thank God that He knows <u>your</u> n even before you ask Him about them.

CRYING OUT TO GOD

xtb · Exodus 2v15-25

Moses was 40 when he ran away from Egypt, and escaped to Midian. *Check out page 8 of your **Mini Map Book** to see where Midian was.*

Look what happened in the next 40 years...

Moses met a family in Midian.

He married and had a son...

...and worked a shepherd.

If you have time, read the full story in Exodus 2v15-22.

Meanwhile, back in Egypt...

READ
Exodus 2v23-25

What happened to Pharaoh? (v23)

he died

That means there was now a <u>new</u> king in Egypt—also called Pharaoh!

The Israelites were still **slaves**. What did they do? (v23)

They cried out to ___God___
(Use yesterday's code.)

At last the Israelites had turned to God for help. But God started answering their prayer long ago!

***Clue:** Moses was <u>40</u> when he went to Midian, and he lived there for <u>40</u> years.*

So Moses was now __80__ years old.

Wow! That means that God started to answer the Israelites' prayer 80 years <u>before</u> they even asked Him!!!

THINK + PRAY

Do you know what your problems or needs will be in a year's time? No!—but God does. God <u>always</u> knows what you need, and always knows what's <u>best</u> for you. That means that you can always trust God to do what's best. Thank God that He is like this.

FIREPOWER

 Exodus 3v1-10

At last it was the right time for God to send Moses back to Egypt...

Moses was looking after the sheep...

...when he saw a bush that was on fire.

But the fire wasn't burning the bush!

When Moses went closer, he heard a voice.

MOSES! MOSES!

Here I am.

I am the God of your father, the God of Abraham, Isaac and Jacob.

Read the Bible verses to find out what else God said to Moses.

READ
Exodus 3v7-10

Shade in the flames with **X**, **Y** or **Z** on them to find out what God was talking to Moses about.

G o d ' s   P r o m i s e

Hundreds of years before, God had made three amazing promises to Abraham, Isaac and Jacob. *Check back to Day 16 to see what they were.*

1 **L** and
2 **C** hildren
3 **B** lessing

Now the time had come for God to keep His promise about the **land**. He was going to rescue His people from Egypt. Who was God going to send to save His people? (v10)

M oses

PRAY **Thank God tha He always ke His promises.**

SD

WHAT'S IN A NAME?

xtb — Exodus 3v10-15

Bible names aren't just names. They also tell you something about the person. The name Moses means 'pull out'. Do you remember who pulled Moses out of the river when he was a baby?

Pharaoh's d*aughter*

Check your answer at the bottom of the page.

God had chosen Moses to lead the Israelites out of Egypt. But Moses knew he couldn't do it on his own.

READ
Exodus 3v10-15

God promised to **be with Moses**. (v12)

What name did God give Himself? (v14)

A = ⇧	
H = ◿	
I = ↑	
M = ↓	
O = ←	
W = ◁	

⇧ ↓ ◁ ◿ ← ↑ ⇧ ↓

am who *I am*

 I AM → What a great name for God!

Follow the maze to find out some of the things this name tells us about God.

 Write the letters in the spaces below.

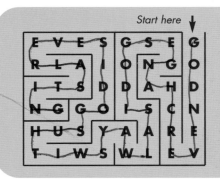

Start here ↓

E V E S G S E G
R L A I O N G O
I T S D D A H D
N G G O I S C N
H U S Y A A R E
T I W S W L E V

G O D N*ever changes*
God is always with us
God is everylastig

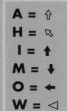 **THINK + PRAY** Think for a while about **God**, the great **I AM**. Then **thank** and **praise** Him for the things listed above.

DAY 23 PLANNING TO GO

Do you or your family have a calendar?
What's planned soon?
—a birthday party?
—a trip to see Granny?
—a visit to the dentist?!

Write your plans here...

Start school

God—the great 'I AM'—is still talking to Moses from the burning bush. He tells Moses about His **plans** to rescue the Israelites.

READ
Exodus 3v16-20

Amazing! God didn't just tell Moses His <u>plans</u>. He also told him the **results**!
*Fill in the gaps, and draw an **arrow** from each plan to its result.*

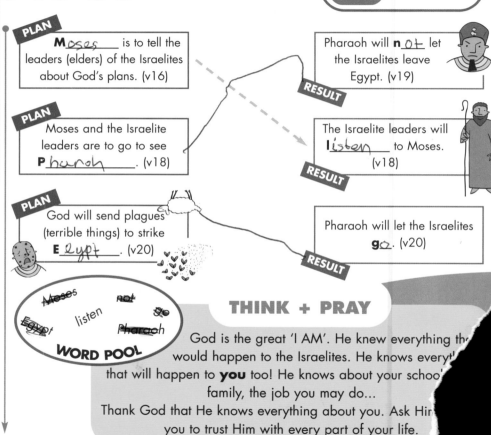

PLAN
M oses is to tell the leaders (elders) of the Israelites about God's plans. (v16)

PLAN
Moses and the Israelite leaders are to go to see P haraoh . (v18)

PLAN
God will send plagues (terrible things) to strike E gypt . (v20)

Pharaoh will **n** ot let the Israelites leave Egypt. (v19)
RESULT

The Israelite leaders will l isten to Moses. (v18)
RESULT

Pharaoh will let the Israelites g o. (v20)
RESULT

WORD POOL
Moses   not   go   Egypt   listen   Pharaoh

THINK + PRAY

God is the great 'I AM'. He knew everything th... would happen to the Israelites. He knows everyt... that will happen to **you** too! He knows about your schoo... family, the job you may do...
Thank God that He knows everything about you. Ask Hi... you to trust Him with every part of your life.

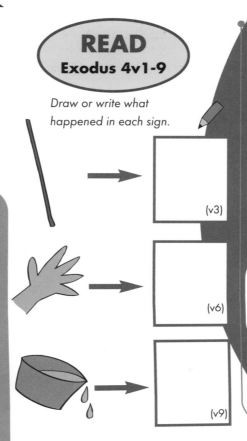

SSSSNAKE SIGN

God is still talking to Moses from the burning bush. God has told Moses to go and speak to the Israelites. But Moses has a worrying question.

what if they don't believe me?

Read his question on the snake.

40 years earlier, when Moses had tried to help the Israelites, they <u>didn't</u> believe he had the right to lead them. Check back to **Day 19** to see what they said...

Who made you our r_____ and J_____ ? (Exodus 2v14)

...it's important that the Israelites know that **God** has chosen Moses to be their leader.

READ
Exodus 4v1-9

Draw or write what happened in each sign.

(v3)

(v6)

(v9)

These three signs showed that Moses really had been sent by God. But there's a far more amazing sign in the New Testament.
Read it on the cross.

Jesus rose from the dead.

Jesus died to save us from our sin—but He didn't stay dead! God brought Him back to life! This sign showed that God accepted Jesus' death as the way for us to be forgiven.

Want to know more?
For a free booklet called **Why did Jesus rise?** write to us at XTB, Blenheim House, 1 Blenheim Road, Epsom, Surrey, KT19 9AP, UK
Or email: alison@thegoodbook.co.uk

PRAY
Thank God for Jesus, who died and rose again as our Rescuer.

DAY 25 EXCUSE ME!

xtb Exodus 4v10-17

God has told Moses what His <u>plans</u> are.
He has told Moses what the <u>results</u> will be.
And He has given Moses three <u>signs</u> to show the Israelites.

But Moses is still worried. This time, his excuse is that he's not good at making speeches...

READ
Exodus 4v10-12

Wow! God reminds Moses that <u>He</u> is the one who gives us the ability to speak. Then what does God promise?
Take the first letter of each picture to find out.

i will help you

Wow! What a fantastic promise! But look at Moses' reply...

Send someone else

READ
Exodus 4v13-17

1 God was angry.
Moses wasn't willing to obey God. So God was angry with him.

2 God was also very patient.
God gave Moses a helper—Aaron his brother. Aaron was a good speaker. He could help Moses to obey God.

THINK + PRAY
Do you sometimes make excuses, instead of obeying God? Tell God you are **sorry** for disobeying Him. Ask Him to hel you to obey Him and not to make excuses.

We'll carry on reading the book of Exodus on Day 46, find out how God keeps His promise to rescue the Israeli

This time,

MATTHEW MATTERS

Two **BIG** questions!

Crack the code to find out what they are.

w h o   i s   J e s u s ?

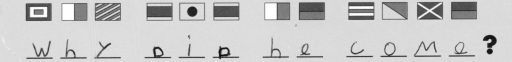

w h y   d i d   h e   c o m e ?

Matthew's book about Jesus helps us to find the answers.

Start now on the next page.

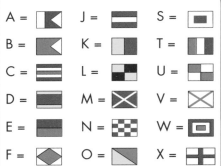

FLAG CODE

DAY 26 ONLY JESUS?
CONTINUED

Where do you live? _Winchester_
Have a think about what it will be like to go back there for a visit once you're grown up.

Today, Jesus goes back to the town where He grew up. Let's see what they think of Him.

READ
Matthew 13v53-54

The people were amazed. What did they say? (v54)

miracles
amazing
wise

He does
m_iracles_

He's w_ise_

He's
a m_azing_

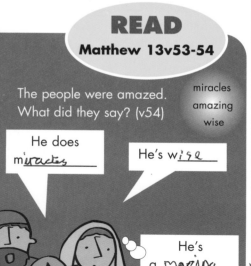

READ
Matthew 13v55-58

What did they know about Jesus? (v55)

His dad's a
c_____ .
His mum is M_____ .
He has 1/2/4 brothers (circle the right number) and some sisters.

Draw one of his tools.

These people knew Jesus' family—and so they decided He couldn't be special. So they got cross!

It's only Jesus! We don't need to listen to him!

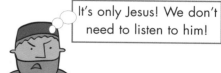

Did you know?

Miracles are like **signposts** pointing to who Jesus is. But these people ignored the amazing things Jesus did and said. They refused to believe that He was God. So He didn't do many miracles in Nazareth. (v58)

Find Nazareth on the map on page 9 of the **Mini Map Book**. Draw a sad face there because they didn't believe.

PRAY

Read v54 again.
Dear God, help me not to ignore the amazing things I read about Jesus. Help me to believe that He really is God. *Amen*

DAY 27 DEAD WRONG

1 At Nazareth they were wrong about Jesus. So is Herod!

READ
Matthew 14v1-2

Who did Herod think Jesus was? (v2)

J_____ the B_____

This is strange, because John is dead!

2 **READ**
Matthew 14v3-12

How horrid!
Underline the right words.

Herod **arrested/thanked** John because John told him that he was disobeying God (by marrying his brother's wife). Herod had a **birthday/Christmas** party and his wife's **friend/daughter** danced for him. He **liked/hated** it and promised her anything she wanted. She asked for John to be **killed/set free**.

3 Herod's actions were very wrong. But what was his biggest problem?

Put the blocks in their correct places to find out.

3 very	6 Jesus	5 about
4 wrong	2 was	1 He

	2	3
	5	6

Herod thought that John the Baptist must have come back to life! He didn't see **who** Jesus really was.

4 Herod hated being told that he had disobeyed God.

THINK + PRAY

How do <u>you</u> react when your parents or someone at church shows you that you are disobeying God? Ask God to help you to listen and change.

FAMOUS FIVE

Find the loaves and fish hidden in the picture.

READ
Matthew 14v13-17

Jesus had crossed the lake to be alone, but a huge crowd followed Him.

What worried the disciples? (v15)

| The football scores | The weather | The crowd needed food |

Who did Jesus say could provide food? (v16)

The **d**_____

But that's impossible! The disciples only had

5 _____ 🥔 and 2 🐟

READ
Matthew 14v18-21

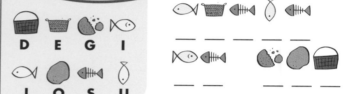			
D	E	G	I
J	O	S	U

Over 5000 people all full up!

Crack the code to find out how!

_____

_____

Did you know?

In the Old Testament God gave food to His people in the desert. Now Jesus shows **He is God** by doing the same thing!

The disciples needed to believe that Jesus is God **and** let that make a difference to their thinking. So must we

PRAY

Dear God, I'm sorry that I forget how powerful You are. Please teach me to You for help to do what You say. Am

DAY 29 SINKING FEELING

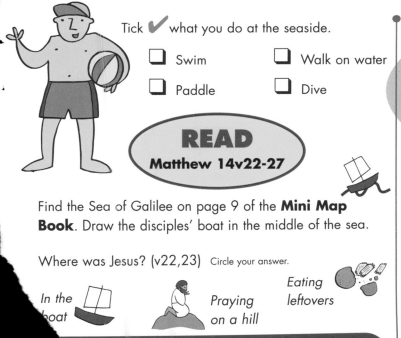

Tick ✔ what you do at the seaside.

☐ Swim   ☐ Walk on water

☐ Paddle   ☐ Dive

READ
Matthew 14v22-27

Find the Sea of Galilee on page 9 of the **Mini Map Book**. Draw the disciples' boat in the middle of the sea.

Where was Jesus? (v22,23) Circle your answer.

In the boat

Praying on a hill

Eating leftovers

...did Jesus get from the hill to the boat? (v25)

_____ on w_____ .

In the **Mini Map Book**, draw Jesus walking on water, towards the boat.

At first, the disciples thought Jesus was a ghost! They thought no-one could walk on water.

READ
Matthew 14v28-32

Peter started sinking because he thought the **wind** was more powerful than **Jesus**.

What had Peter and the other disciples forgotten?
*Cross out all the **A**, **B** & **C**'s on the wave.*

ABJCEASBCUASBCAIBSCABGAOBDAB

Jesus wants the disciples to believe that He is God and that they can trust Him. **Read verse 33.** They are starting to believe, but they still have a lot to learn!

PRAY Dear God, please help me to remember how powerful Jesus is. *Amen*

DAY 30 IT'S JESUS!

Remember **Nazareth**? (*Day 26*)

 Um?

They thought Jesus was just an ordinary man!

 Now I remember!

Write two things Jesus did to show that they were wrong.

 Jesus fed
+
Jesus walked

Today Jesus meets people who <u>know</u> He's no ordinary man!

READ
Matthew 14v34-36

The story's muddled up! Put numbers in the boxes ☐ to show the right order.

Look, it's Jesus! ☐

Come! Jesus will heal you. ☐

Everyone who touched Jesus was healed! ☐

Jesus arrived in Gennesaret. ☐

What does this story tell us about Jesus?

Put a ☺ by the right answers and cross out the others.

He's caring.   He's unkind.

He can't help.   He's more powerful than sickness.

At Gennesaret they believed that Jesus could **heal** and that He **cared**. They were right!

Find Gennesaret on the map on page 9 of your **Mini Map Book**. Draw a happy face there. ☺

PRAY Thank God that Jesus is caring and powerful.

Don't forge'
Jesus came
som
spe

31 UPSIDE DOWN

Whose commands are top?

Write the words the right way up.

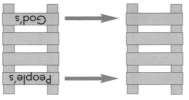

God's commands are top! Read how the religious leaders got things upside down...

READ
Matthew 15v1-7

Fill the gaps with these word

wash
hands
human
hearts
words

The Pharisees were cross! The disciples were breaking one of the **their** commands.

...hat was it? (v2)

...idn't **w**_____ their **h**_____ in a special way.

They a...
W...

The Pharisees thought this made people O.K. with ...d. *Discover what Jesus thinks tomorrow.*

Whose commands are the Pharisees disobeying? (v3) **G**_____

Whose teaching **do** they follow? (v3)

theirs!
should be top, not
God's commands
That's upside down!

READ
Matthew 15v7-9

Isaiah was an Old Testament prophet (a messenger from God). What did he say about people like the Pharisees? (v8-9)

They honour God with their **w**_____ . BUT that's all! Their **h**_____ are far from God. They treat **h**_____ commands the same as God's.

THINK + PRAY Are God's commands top in your life? Ask God to help you to obey **Him**.

AY 32 INSIDE OUT

Unravel the lines.

God's commands
Pharisees' commands

OUTSIDE
UPSIDE
INSIDE
OFFSIDE

The Pharisees worried about what they were like on the **outside**. But it's what we're like **inside** that matters to God!

As we saw yesterday, the Pharisees thought the disciples were 'unclean' because they hadn't washed their hands in a special way.

Read round the hand to see what **unclean** means.

Separated from God

READ
Matthew 15v10-11

What <u>really</u> separates us from God? (v11)

☐ What goes into us from outside
☑ What comes out of us from inside

✔ *Tick the right answer*

READ
Matthew 15v15-20

Where do the things that separate us from God come from? (v18)

The **h**eart

Read the red words. Then finish the arrows to show where they come from.

Lying
Stealing
Bad thoughts
Saying nasty things

---

xtb Matthew 15v10-20

THINK SPOT

The Pharisees worried about what they were like on the outside. But we can't wash away things like these red words. They come from inside, from our hearts. *Crack the code to find out who <u>can</u> make our hearts clean.*

❤ ❤
E J
❤ ❤
S U

J E S U S

THINK + PRAY

Being forgiven is like being washe_ clean on the i_ *Thank Jes_* for you_ _s for dying _so that you can be fo_give_ _rgiven.

DAY 33 **DOG FOOD**

Today Jesus travels to a different area. Write down every other letter to see who lives there.

Start with G

GPEONPTSITLAERSS G e n t i l e s

> The Jews were God's special people. Everyone else was called a **Gentile**.

Find the Gentile area on page 10 of your **Mini Map Book**. *Draw Jesus there.*

READ
Matthew 15v21-27

Why does the Gentile woman need help? (v22)

> Her daughter has a **d e m o n**

Demons are evil spirits. They are God's enemies.

What does Jesus say? (v24)

> I've come to help the lost **s_____** of **I_____**

Jesus must go to the Jews **first**.
He says that going to the Gentiles first would be like giving the children's food to dogs!

The woman agrees! But what does she say? (v27)

> Even dogs get _____

READ verse 28

This woman had great faith. Follow the arrows to see why.

She believed
too ← for Gentiles
Jesus had come

And she was right!

PRAY Thank God that Jesus came for **EVERYONE.**

DAY 34 FOOD FOR ALL

 Cross out any letters that appear **three times** to see who God made a promise about in the Old Testament.

g e n t i l e s

READ
Matthew 15v32-39

Where will we find enough food to feed this crowd?

In the Old Testament, God promised that many Gentiles would believe in Him and belong to His special people.

READ
Matthew 15v29-31

What's strange about the disciple's question?

- ☐ There's a shop around the corner.
- ☐ No-one's hungry.
- ☑ They know Jesus fed 5000 people!

Jesus fed this crowd of Gentiles just as He had fed a Jewish crowd. His disciples should have believed!

Wow! Look how God is keeping His promise! These Gentiles shared in the amazing things Jesus did. They had the chance to believe in Him too.

How many Gentiles came to Jesus? (v30) (Circle) your answer.

1   5

A large crowd

Jesus healed many who were sick. How did the crowd respond? (v31)

They p raised   G od

PRAY Jesus wants **everyone** to know about Him. Ask God to give you the courage to tell people about Jesus.

Draw lines to show what each sign points to.

Dark clouds .... **Flu**

Sore throat .... **A party**

Buying balloons and a cake .... **Rain**

The Pharisees were good at understanding some signs, but rubbish at others! Today they've teamed up with some Sadducees (another religious group) to ask Jesus for a sign.

READ
Matthew 16v1-4

Tick ✔ the signs they **do** understand and cross ✗ the signs they **don't**. (v2-3)

Signs about weather	✔
Signs about Jesus	✗

The Pharisees and Sadducees understand weather signs, but refuse to believe signs showing that Jesus is God! What is the only sign they will get? (v4)

 The sign of **J** _Jesus_

D   E   I

R   S

Crack the code to see what the sign of Jonah is.

Jonah was swallowed by a fish, but returned safely to land after three days.

Jesus will _d i e_ but will _R i s e_ again after three days.

The Pharisees don't need **more** signs. They need to **believe** the signs God gives!

JESUS

PRAY We're reading about those signs in Matthew's book. Ask God to help you to believe them.

Have you ever made bread? **Yes**

A **tiny bit** of something called yeast spreads through the **whole** loaf to make it rise! Remember that for later!

READ
Matthew 16v5-12

What was Jesus warning about? (v6)

The **y** _?_ of the **P** _?_

What had the disciples forgotten? (v5)

Draw your answer

The disciples think Jesus is talking about bread! They're worried because they forgot it!

The disciples shouldn't worry about bread! They should remember **who** Jesus is!

Draw a line from the loaves to the number of people Jesus fed. (See v9 & 10)

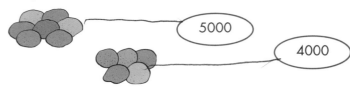

5000

4000

Jesus is God! He can provide bread! They need to trust Him!

But Jesus was talking about something more important than bread. What was Jesus warning about? (*Take the first letter of each picture to find out.*)

The _Teaching_ of the religious leaders.

<u>Wrong</u> teaching, from religious leaders who wouldn't believe Jesus, was spreading everywhere—like yeast. The disciples mustn't believe it.

PRAY

Pray that you would **trust** Jesus to look after you and only believe **truth** about Him.

DAY 37 JESUS JIGSAW

1 Matthew has been building up a picture for us of **who Jesus is**.

But the disciples can't put the picture together. Until, suddenly, Peter slots in the final piece...

READ
Matthew 16v13-17

2 People said Jesus was a **prophet**—someone to tell them about God.

Who does **Peter** say Jesus is? (v16)

The _____ ,
the Son of the living God.

Peter is right! God helped him to see that Jesus is the Christ (the Messiah).

3 Read the chain from the middle to see what **Christ** and **Messiah** mean.

H O S
C G E
G S D N
N I K

Gods chosen King

4 In the Old Testament, God promised His people a **King** who would **rescue** them. Now He's come, and He's God Himself!!

READ
Matthew 16v18-20

5 What's Jesus going to build? (v18)

His church

Many people will believe! They'll be called the church. And Peter will teach them what pleases Jesus.

6 Find Caesarea Philippi on page 11 of your **Mini Map Book.** *Draw a **crown** there because Jesus is the promised King.*

PRAY **Praise Jesus for being King!**

DAY 38 ROYAL RESCUE

What would you like about being King or Queen?

crown

Let's see what King Jesus' plans are...

READ
Matthew 16v21-23

Use the red words to fill in the gaps.

~~Jerusalem~~   ~~die~~

~~suffer~~   ~~never!~~

Where must Jesus go? (v21)

 J_erusalem

What will happen?

Jesus will s_uffer and d_ie

Surprised? Peter was! What did he say?

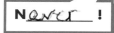

Never !

This should **never** happen to Jesus!

Find the red words in the wordsearch. *Some are written backwards!*

M E L A S U R E J
E I D S U F F E R
N E V E R ! S I N

Where did Peter get his ideas about what Jesus should do? (v23)   ✔ *Tick the answer*

God	
People	✓

Peter should have trusted **God's** plans, but he was full of human ideas instead.

Jesus was the <u>rescuing</u> King. Dying was the **only** way to rescue us from our biggest problem.

Find the leftover word in the wordsearch, to see what that problem is.

S i n

Sin is doing what **we** want instead of what **God** wants. Sin separates us from God. *If you're not sure how Jesus rescues us from sin, check out **Judge and Rescuer** after Day 13.*

Draw a cross ✝ by Jerusalem on page 11 of the **Mini Map Book**, because Jesus **had to** die. *Now draw an arrow from the crown you drew yesterday to the cross in Jerusalem.*

PRAY **Thank God that Jesus died to rescue you!**

DAY 39 FOLLOW THE LEADER

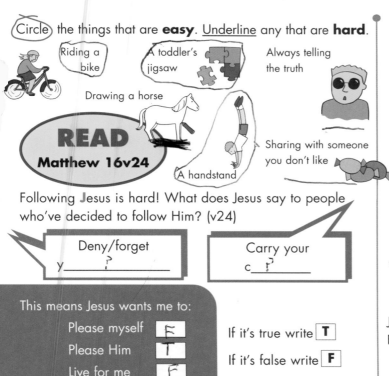

Circle the things that are **easy**. Underline any that are **hard**.

Riding a bike

A toddler's jigsaw

Always telling the truth

Drawing a horse

A handstand

Sharing with someone you don't like

READ
Matthew 16v24

Following Jesus is hard! What does Jesus say to people who've decided to follow Him? (v24)

Deny/forget
y_____?

Carry your
c__?

This means Jesus wants me to:

Please myself	F
Please Him	T
Live for me	F
Live for Him (+ even die for Him)	T

If it's true write **T**

If it's false write **F**

Answers at the bottom of the page.

That's hard! It's also best!

READ
Matthew 16v25-28

The World

Life and Soul

Soul = the part of us that goes on living for ever

What's the best thing to have? (v26) *Draw a line from the answer to 1st prize.*

1st Prize

Life's best! Not life now, but living **forever** with Jesus. That's better than owning the whole world!

Who can give eternal life?
Copy the red letters (in order). J e s u s

Jesus gives eternal life to those who follow Him. Following Jesus is hard, but best!

PRAY **It's hard following Jesus! Ask Him for help.**

DAY 40 PEAK PREVIEW

Look at what the disciples (and we!) have learnt:
1 Jesus is the promised **King** (Day 37)
2 Jesus had come to **die** (Day 38)
3 Following Jesus is **hard** (Day 39)

That's a lot for them to take in!

Now Jesus encourages three of his friends with a peak preview on a mountain…

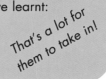

READ
Matthew 17v1-8

How did Jesus change? (v2)

His _body_ was like the sun and His _clothes_ were dazzlingly white.

Who appeared with Jesus? (v3)

M _oses_   **E** _lijah_

Moses and Elijah served God in the Old Testament. *We'll go back to the story of Moses on Day 46.*

Not surprisingly Peter's excited—but he needs to realise that Jesus is <u>far greater</u> than Moses or Elijah.

What did God the Father say about Jesus from the cloud? (v5)

This is my **S** _on_ , with whom I am
p _leased_ . **L** _ove_ to Him!

Six days earlier, Jesus told His disciples He was going to die. They didn't want to believe Him. But now what did God tell them to do? (v5)

L ___?___ **to Jesus.**

The disciples have just had a glimpse of how **great** Jesus is. They must <u>listen</u> to Him and <u>believe</u> what He says. *Replace the missing pieces to see what they particularly need to accept.*

1	2	3	4	5		2		4
J H	e g d	SS I	U T e	S O		E A D		U T E

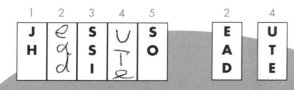

PRAY Even though Jesus is so **great**, He died for you and me! Thank Him!

DAY 41 TOP SECRET

Draw Jesus and three disciples coming down the mountain.

They have just seen how **great** Jesus is. Imagine telling people!

READ
Matthew 17v9

When can they tell everyone? (v9)

- ❑ Never
- ❑ Now
- ❑ After Jesus had risen from the dead

Read round the soldier's shield to see why they must wait.

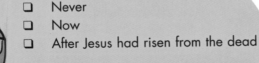

The people wanted the wrong kind of rescue.

If the disciples spoke now, people would try to make Jesus a **human** king to rescue them from **human** enemies (the Romans). But Jesus came to rescue us from the real problem—**sin**.

READ
Matthew 17v10-13

In the Old Testament, God promised that a prophet like Elijah would come just before the rescuing King. And he **had** come.

Who was it? (v13)

J_____ the **B**_____

But the people didn't recognise him! God kept His promise, but many Jews refused to believe. They treated John badly, and would do the same to Jesus.

THINK+PRAY

Most people had the wrong idea about Jesus. That's true today as well. Many people think that Jesus wasn't very special, or didn't even exist! They don't understand that He is our rescuing King. **Pray for your friends.** Ask God to help you to tell them about Jesus.

DAY 42 POWER SUPPLY

Take the first letter of each picture to find three words from today's story.

d i s c i p l e s

f a i t h   J e s u s

Look out for these words as you read today's story.

READ
Matthew 17v14-21

The man's son had a demon. The boy was in danger.

Who tried to help him but couldn't? (v16)

The d _eciples_

Why couldn't the disciples heal him? (v20)

They didn't have f _aith_

They're just like everyone else! They still don't believe.

Who did heal the boy? (v18) *Jesus*

Jesus is very powerful! *Cross out the **M**s, **N**s and **O**s to see who that power was available to.*

The Disciples

The disciples should have asked for **Jesus'** power to heal the boy.

What is possible for people who have faith? (v21)

Circle the answer   (Everything)   Most things   Nothing

PRAY
We can always trust in God's great power to help us to do what He says. Ask Him for that trust.

READ
Matthew 17v22-23
Don't forget what Jesus is about to do!

DAY 43 FISHY MONEY

Who pays to enter a theme park?

Circle your answer The owner's son **The general public** *(circled)*

It would be crazy to ask the son to pay!

Something similar happens in today's story...

READ
Matthew 17v24-27

What tax were they collecting? (v24)

The t_emples_ tax

The temple tax was money collected for the temple.

Did Peter think Jesus should pay? (v25)

Shade in the coin with the right answer

 Yes

What did Jesus ask Peter? (v25)

> Who do kings collect money from? Their s_ons_ or o_ther_ people?

Other people of course! **Sons** don't pay their fathers!

Crack the code to see what Jesus is saying about Himself.

D G N O S

I am G O d S
S O N

Jesus is God's Son. It's crazy to ask Him to pay for the temple. It belongs to His Father!

In fact, the whole world belongs to God —including all the fish!

Draw what Peter found in the fish's mouth. (v27)

Wow! Everything belongs to God— so He provided the money for the tax!

Praise Jesus! He is God's Son. The whole world belongs to Him.

DAY 44 ROYAL PARDON

How easy is it to forgive?

Tick your answer

| It depends! | Hard! | Easy |

READ
Matthew 18v21-22

Peter thinks he should forgive someone **seven** times.

How many times does Jesus say? (v22)

Jesus means there should be **no limit!** Let's see why.

READ
Matthew 18v23-26

One servant owed the king millions of pounds!

Could he pay it back? (v25)

No! His family would have to be slaves!

What did he say to the king? (v26)

PLEASE WAIT!
I'll pay you back _____

READ
Matthew 18v27

The king let him go. He didn't have to pay anything! *Draw the servant's face!*

Use the pictures to see what Jesus' story means.

The king is like 👑 _____

The servant is like 🙂 _____

The money the servant owes is like ☹ _____

👑 _____ forgives **all** our ☹ _____

👑 **God**

🙂 **Us**

☹ **Sin**

God forgives all our sin because Jesus died as our Rescuer. We just have to ask!

PRAY **Thank God for forgiving us without limit.**

DAY 45 ROYAL REBUKE

What was Peter's question yesterday?

How many times should I **f**_____ someone?

Jesus said there should be **no limit!**

Remember the story about the servant who owed millions of pounds? The king said he didn't have to pay it back! *Now read what happened next...*

READ
Matthew 18v28-30

Who owed the servant money? (v28)

Another servant owed him a few pounds—and he put him in prison!

How different is that from the way the king treated him?

Underline the answer

Not very different

Completely different

READ
Matthew 18v31-35

The servant should have acted like the king. But he didn't—and was thrown into **jail**!

Draw his face.

Use the pictures to see what Jesus' story means.

♔ ____ has forgiven 大 ____	♔ **God**
without limit.	大 **Us**
So we should forgive 大大 _____	大大 **Others**
without limit.	

 THINK SPOT

God's forgiveness is amazing! But when <u>we</u> don't forgive it shows that we don't understand how much **God** has forgiven **us**.

PRAY **Ask God to help you to forgive others without limit.**

DAY 46 WHO'S THE BOSS?

Read the Hieroglyphics to find a BIG question.

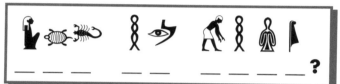

_ _ _   _ _ _   _ _ _ _ _ **?**

This is the **BIG** question in Exodus. The king of Egypt is called Pharaoh. He <u>thinks</u> he's the most important person around. But he needs to learn the real truth!

The <u>real</u> King is _ _ _

D=

G=

H=

I=

K=

N=

O=

S=

W=

Moses and his brother Aaron have gone to see Pharaoh. They have a message from God.

READ
Exodus 5v1-2

What was God's message to Pharaoh? (v1)

Let _ _   _ _ _ _ _ _   _ _

This is God's message. The Israelites are **His** people. Pharaoh must obey God.

But look at Pharaoh's proud answer:

> **I do n _ _ know the LORD;**
> **and I will n _ _ let Israel go.** (v2)

The scene is set for God to show Pharaoh who's <u>really</u> King!

More on the next page.

The story so far...

- The Israelites are **slaves** in Egypt.
- God has promised to **rescue** them.
- He has chosen **Moses** to be their leader.

Exodus 5v1-21

The XTB Guide to Brick Building

1 Take one large dollop of mud
2 Chop straw into little bits
3 Mix mud and straw together
4 Squash into a brick shape
5 Leave to dry in the hot sun

Ingredients
Mud
Straw
Sun
Slaves

The Israelites worked very hard making bricks for the Egyptians. But Pharaoh decided that they were **lazy**, and gave new instructions to his slave-drivers…

Don't give the Israelites straw any more. Make them get their own!

But make sure they make just as many bricks as before!

So the Israelites searched all over Egypt for straw. But this made their work slower…

Where are today's bricks? You haven't done enough! Why not?

The Israelite foremen went to see Pharaoh. It's not our fault! We can't make bricks without straw!

But Pharaoh refused to help. You're lazy! You won't be given any straw!

You can read this story for yourself in Exodus 5v6-21

THINK SPOT

The Israelites were in a tough situation. It was rotten being slaves—and now things had got even worse!

It <u>looked</u> like Pharaoh could do what he liked. He seemed to be in charge of everything. **But he wasn't!**

Pharaoh (and the Israelites) were about to see that **God** is the <u>real</u> King!

PRAY

The book of Exodus shows us that God is the **King of Kings**. Ask God to help you to get to know Him better as you read Exodus.

A BROKEN PROMISE?

 Exodus 5v22-6v8

God had promised to **rescue** the Israelites—but instead things seemed to be getting worse! Did this mean that God wasn't going to keep His promise?

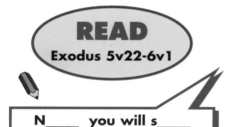

READ
Exodus 5v22-6v1

N____ you will s____ what I w____ do. (v1)

God hadn't forgotten His promises (called the **covenant**). Instead, He was going to make Pharaoh <u>drive</u> the Israelites out of Egypt!

READ
Exodus 6v2-8

Look at the great things God told Moses.

> I am **the LORD**. (v2)
> I have **heard** the groaning of the Israelites. (v5)
> I have **remembered** my covenant promise. (v5)
> I will **bring** you out of Egypt. (v6)
> I will **free** you from slavery. (v6)
> I will **give** you the promised land. (v8)

Find the <u>red</u> words in the wordsearch. Some are written backwards.

I	F	R	E	E	D	R	A	E	H
R	E	M	E	M	B	E	R	E	D
B	R	I	N	G	W	E	V	I	G
T	H	E	L	O	R	D	I	L	L

Copy the leftover letters here (in order).

__ __ __ __ __ __

 THINK SPOT

God didn't say "I'm hoping to..." or "I'll probably...". He said **"I will"**.

God may allow suffering and pain, but it never interferes with His plans. Nothing that Pharaoh (or any other person) does, can stop God!

THINK + PRAY

Even when things look bad, nothing can stop God's plans. **Thank God that He is always in control.**

GOD'S MIGHTY HAND!

xtb Exodus 6v28-7v5

God has promised Moses that He **will** rescue the Israelites. But Moses is still worried.

Why would Pharaoh listen to me?

Look at God's fantastic answer:

READ
Exodus 6v28-7v5

PRAY **Thank God that He is the King of Kings.**

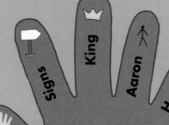

*Use these **words** and **pictures** to fill in the gaps.*

Signs / King / Aaron / Heart / Hand

1. Moses isn't good at making speeches. So **A**_____ will speak for him. (*Aaron will be like a prophet, one of God's messengers.*)

2. But Pharaoh's **h**_____ will be hard. This means he won't listen to Moses.

3. God will do miraculous **s**_____ and wonders.

4. God will stretch out His **h**_____ against Egypt, and rescue the Israelites.

Read **verse 5** again. This doesn't mean a giant hand in the sky! It means that God would show His great power.

When the people see how God rescues the Israelites, they will know that He is the LORD, the real **K**____

DAY 49 STICKS AND SNAKES

Flashback...

When God was speaking to Moses from the burning bush, He gave Moses three signs. They showed that Moses really had been sent by God.

Do you remember what happened when Moses threw down his staff?

Check Exodus 4v3-4 or Day 24 of XTB if you're not sure.

Write or draw your answer.

Now it was time for Moses and Aaron to show Pharaoh a sign...

READ
Exodus 7v6-13

Cross out the wrong words.

Aaron's staff turned into a **cake/rake/snake**. But Pharaoh wasn't impressed. He called in his **magicians/clowns/servants**. Each one threw down his **hat/gloves/staff** and it turned into a snake too. But Aaron's staff **tickled/swallowed/painted** theirs! But Pharaoh didn't **watch/thank/listen to** Moses, just as God had said.

THINK SPOT

For a moment, it looked like the magicians were just as powerful as God. But then Aaron's staff <u>swallowed</u> theirs! **Nobody** is as powerful as God!

Cross out every **second word** to find some important words from verse 13.

JUST TOAST AS WITH THE BUTTER LORD AND HAD MARMALADE SAID

J_____ ____ ____ _____
_____ _____

God had already told Moses what would happen. (*We read about it on Day 23.*) God had told Moses that He would do amazing miracles, but that Pharaoh wouldn't listen. It was all happening **just as God said**.

PRAY
Thank God that His words always come true.

PATTERNS, PLAGUES & PRAYERS

Exodus
7v17 & 10v1-2

Pattern Puzzle:

Only two patterns are exactly the same. Which two?

A   **B**   **C**   **D**

E   **F**   **G**   **H**

Pattern Plagues:

As we saw yesterday, Pharaoh refused to listen to God's message. So now God would send **ten plagues** on Egypt—ten terrible miracles. The first nine plagues came in a **pattern**. They came in three <u>triplets</u>. Each triplet showed something amazing about God.

Plagues 1, 2 & 3 ——————▶ You can't beat **God**.

Plagues 4, 5 & 6 ——▶ The Israelites are **God's** people.

Plagues 7, 8 & 9 ——————▶ **God** is the GREATEST.

Look out for this pattern over the next few days.

Answer: Patterns D and F are the same.

Pattern Purpose:

What was the purpose of the plagues?
Take the first letter of each picture to find out.

By this you will know that

____ ____ ____ ____ ____

 READ **Exodus 7v17 & 10v1-2** to check your answer.

Pattern Prayers:

Pharaoh and the Egyptians needed to know that God is the Lord, the real King. So do many countries today. Each day we will pray for one country, and ask God to show the people and leaders of that country that **He** is the real King.

Which country do <u>you</u> live in?

 WORLD PRAYER Pray for the leaders of your country. Ask God to help them to make good and fair decisions. Ask God to help them to understand that He is the King of Kings, and that the Bible will show them the best way to lead the country.

DAY 51 ONE TWO THREE

 Exodus 7v20-24

Ancient Egypt (the land of Pharaoh and the Pyramids) was about to see **astounding** things happen. God was going to show everyone that **He** is the real King.

Read the Hieroglyphics to see what happened.

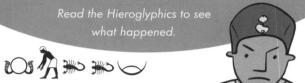

_ _ _ _ _ _

_ _ _ _ _ _

The biggest river in Egypt is the Nile. Early one morning, God sent Moses and Aaron to the Nile to meet Pharaoh. They went to warn Pharaoh about the first plague.

READ
Exodus 7v20-24

A= ☥
B= ◖◗
D= ⌣
E= 𓅿
F= 𓅆
G= 𓊪
L= 𓀃
N= 𓀔
O= 𓆙
R= 𓎼
S= 𓂀
T= 𓃠

What happened?

The water turned to **b**_____ (v20)

The fish all **d**_____ (v21)

The river **s**_____ really bad. (v21)

But did Pharaoh listen to Moses? (v22) **Yes / No**

The next two plagues were terrible too. **Frogs** came pouring out of the Nile, and hopped EVERYWHERE! Then the dust turned into crawling, biting **Gnats**!

Find the River Nile on page 12 of your **Mini Map Book**. Colour the Nile red to show that it turned to blood. Then draw loads of frogs hopping out of it.

WORLD PRAYER The Capital of modern **Egypt** is Cairo. It is one of the largest cities in Africa. About half the people in Cairo are very poor and live in slums. **Thank God** for the Christians who go into the slums to help the poor. **Ask God** to help them show the poor that God loves them and that He is their real King.

DAY 52 YOU CAN'T BEAT GOD!

Who do you think won each trophy?
Follow the lines to find out.

Embroidery competition — 1st

Doughnut eating contest — 1st

20 mile swim

Pharaoh's magicians thought **they** could compete with **God**!

1 **Water turned to blood.**
   The magicians turned water into blood too.

2 **Frogs everywhere.**

   The magicians made frogs appear too.

3 **Dust became gnats.**

   The magicians could not produce gnats!

READ
Exodus 8v16-19

Who did the magicians say had changed the dust into gnats? (v19)

But Pharaoh still wouldn't listen!

Look back to the Frog Plague to find out what these plagues were showing about God.

READ
Exodus 8v8-15

xtb Exodus 8v8-19

Moses said the frogs would leave at a time chosen by Pharaoh. **Why?** (v10)

So that you may know there is

__ __ __ __ __ like God.

Will Pharaoh learn who God really is? *We'll find out more tomorrow...*

WORLD PRAYER

The river Nile runs through **Sudan**, which has been hit by war and famine for many years. Sudan split into two countries in 2011. Lots of the Christians had to move south, and now very few live in the northern country. **Ask God** to help them to keep following Jesus, even when that's very hard, and to tell other people about Jesus.

DAY 53 FOUR FIVE SIX

Waiter, what's this fly doing in my soup?

I think it's backstroke, Sir!

Imagine 20 flies in your soup! And more landing on your nose and crawling through your hair! That's what the next plague was like...

READ
Exodus 8v20-24

Where did God say the flies would go? (v21)

On **P**_____

On the **E**_____

In the Egyptian **h**_____

houses
Egyptians
Pharaoh
Goshen

But there would be **no flies** in **G**_____ , where the Israelites lived!

Check out the map on page 12 of your **Mini Map Book**. Colour in the area of Goshen, where the Israelites lived.

The plague of flies was the beginning of the next triplet of plagues—numbers 4, 5 & 6. Unjumble the letters to see what they were.

SLIEF

F_____

SLAMINA

A_____

LIBOS

B_____

More about these plagues tomorrow...

WORLD PRAYER

There are over 800 different groups of people living in **Papua New Guinea** (PNG), and each group speaks its own language! Everyone also speaks "Tok Pisin", a kind of simple English. My friend Rosie works in PNG. She teaches women there about Jesus, and helps them understand the Bible. **Pray** for Rosie, and other Christian missionaries in PNG. **Ask God** to help them to tell people the great news about Jesus.

DAY 54 GOD'S SPECIAL PEOPLE

xtb Exodus 9v1-7

Where might you see this sign?

a) Your classroom door.
b) Your brother's bedroom.
c) A nuclear power plant.

Warning signs help us to know what not to do or where not to go. God gave Pharaoh a warning about what would happen if he <u>didn't</u> let the Israelites go.

READ
Exodus 9v1-5

So far, Pharaoh hasn't listened to God. Do you think he will obey God this time?

Yes / No / Maybe

READ
Exodus 9v6-7

Pharaoh <u>didn't</u> listen. So God's words came true.

None
All
Obey

A_____ of the Egyptians' animals died.

N_____ of the Israelites' animals died.

But Pharaoh still wouldn't _____ God!

Spot six differences between this Egyptian and Israelite.

Plague Six (Exodus 9v8-12)

God showed Pharaoh that the Israelites were **different** from the Egyptians. There were <u>no flies</u> in Goshen. The Israelite cattle <u>didn't</u> die. And the Israelites didn't get boils either!

Why? Because they were **God's** special people.

More tomorrow...

WORLD PRAYER

Haiti is the poorest country in the western world. Many people practise voodoo, which involves worshipping spirits. It often leaves people full of fear. One way the people hear about Jesus is through Christian radio stations. **Ask God** to help people in Haiti to understand what they hear on the Christian radio stations, and to learn about God's love for them.

DAY 55 SEVEN EIGHT NINE

xtb · Exodus 9v13-19

Which blue line is l-o-n-g-e-s-t?

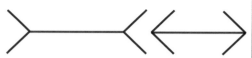

Check your answer below.

In the puzzle it's hard to see which line is longest. The next three plagues showed who is the **greatest**. But it wasn't hard to see the answer. God made it VERY CLEAR!

READ
Exodus 9v13-19

God told Pharaoh <u>why</u> the plagues were happening:

So that you may know that there is _____ like me in all the world. (v14)

Take the first letter of each picture to see what the next three plagues were.

_____

_____

_____

Find these words in the wordsearch. *Some are written backwards.*

G	S	S	E	N	K	R	A	D
R	E	A	T	E	L	I	A	H
L	O	C	U	S	T	S	S	T

What do the leftover letters spell?

G _ _ _ _ _ _ _ _ _

God made it very clear that **He** is the greatest. *Tomorrow we'll see how Pharaoh reacts...*

WORLD PRAYER

India is full of temples and shrines. The people are very religious. Most are Hindus, but there are many other religions too. Christian missionaries have worked in India for hundreds of years, and now almost 6% of Indians are Christians. **Ask God** to help them see how important it is to tell other people about Jesus. Pray that Christians in India will tell others the great news about the <u>one God</u>, who loves them.

Answer: Both lines are the same length.

DAY 56 GOD'S THE GREATEST!

Exodus 9v15-21

Close your eyes, and imagine what Plagues 7, 8 & 9 were like. The **worst hailstorm** ever. **More locusts** than ever seen before. Then **so dark** that the darkness could be <u>felt</u>! These were all sent by the GREATEST KING—God Himself.

Let's go back to the plague of hail to see how Pharaoh and his officials reacted...

READ
Exodus 9v19-21

Some of Pharaoh's officials **believed** God's words. Others **ignored** Him.

outside   inside
believed
ignored

Those who **b**_____ God brought their slaves and animal **i**_____ .
Those who **i**_____ God left their slaves and animals **o**_____ .

The hail came—just as God had said. And all those who were left outside were killed—just as God had said.

After each plague, Pharaoh had a choice to make. He could **obey** God, and let the Israelites go. Or he could **ignore** God, and refuse.

Follow the lines to see what Pharaoh did.

3 times

4 times

2 times

Pharaoh wouldn't listen.

Pharaoh said Yes, but that only <u>some</u> could go.

Pharaoh said Yes, but then changed his mind.

Now look at what God said about Pharaoh...

READ
Exodus 9v15-16

Wow! It was God who made Pharaoh the king of Egypt, so that <u>everyone</u> in the world would know about God and His great power! That includes **you and me!**

WORLD PRAYER

In **Romania** young people are more likely to become Christians than anyone else. Some go on Christian camps in their school holidays where they learn from the Bible. Pray for these young people. **Ask God** to help churches in Romania teach children and young people about God and show them how important He is.

HARD HEARTED

xtb Exodus 11v1-8

*Colour in all the shapes with **A**, **B** or **C** in them.*

Pharaoh's heart was **hard**. But how did it get that way?

During the first plagues we are told that Pharaoh hardened his heart himself. (E.g. Exodus 8v15 & 32)

But later on the Bible tells us that 'the LORD hardened Pharaoh's heart.' (E.g. Exodus 10v20 & 27)

Why did God do that?

Pharaoh had <u>already chosen</u> to reject God—so God made him what he had **chosen** to be.

Pharaoh's heart was now rock hard. But the last plague would change everything...

READ
Exodus 11v1-8

What a terrible plague. The eldest son (the firstborn) of every <u>Egyptian</u> family will die. So will the firstborn of all the Egyptian cattle. But the eldest sons of the <u>Israelites</u> will be kept safe. (*We'll find out more about that in the next few days.*)

WORLD PRAYER

The plagues showed God's great power to the Egyptians. They saw that He is the LORD—the King of Kings.

*Turn to the World Map on page 6 of your **Mini Map Book**.*

Our world is full of people who don't know that God is their LORD. Some have hardened their hearts, like Pharaoh. Other have never even heard about the one true God who loves them. But there are also <u>Christians</u> living in every country of the world. **Ask God** to help those Christians, wherever they live, to tell others about Jesus. Ask God to help <u>you</u> to tell your friends about Jesus too.

DAY 58 **PASSOVER**

Match each person with what they are going to do.

Football match

Dinner party

Scottish dance

Scuba diving

Did you find one pair hard to match up? In today's verses the Israelites are told to dress in their travelling clothes, each with a cloak and staff. But then they must stay <u>inside</u> for a meal!

Read the verses to find out more.

READ
Exodus 12v1-11

quickly
perfect • roasted
staff • sides

Special Instructions (Fill in the gaps)

• Each family is to choose a lamb. It must be **p**_____.

• Put blood on the **s**_____ and tops of the doorframes.

• Eat the lamb **r**_____ — not raw or boiled.

• Make sure you have your cloak and a **s**_____ .

• Eat **q**_____ !

Exodus 12v1-13

This final plague is called the **Passover**. Read the next two verses to see why.

READ
Exodus 12v12-13

The Lord will pass through Egypt. Every firstborn son and animal will die. But when God sees the blood on the doorposts of a house, He will **p**_____ **o**_____ that house. Everyone inside it will be kept safe.

God told the Israelites exactly what to do to stay safe. Do you think they will obey Him?

We'll find out more tomorrow.

PRAY

Obeying God is <u>always</u> the best and safest thing to do. Ask God to help you to obey Him, even when that's hard.

PS Why were the Israelites to wear their travelling clothes? Because they would be leaving Egypt **very soon...**

DAY 59 THE PASSOVER LAMB

Moses gave God's instructions to the Israelites. They were to kill the Passover **lamb**, and put its blood on the sides and **top** of their doorframes. Then they were to stay **inside**, in safety. When God saw the **blood** on their houses, He would pass **over** their homes. That night would be one the Israelites would **never** forget. Each year at Passover time, they were to remind their **children** of its amazing events.

You can read this for yourself in Exodus 12v21-27

Fit all of the underlined words into the puzzle below to discover a hidden word.

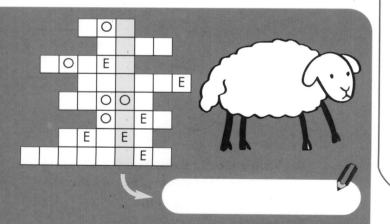

READ
Exodus 12v28-30

Did the Israelites obey God? (v28)

Yes / No

That night something or someone died in **every house**. In the Egyptian homes it was the oldest son who died. But in the Israelite homes the oldest son was kept safe. The Passover lamb died **instead**, in his place.

That means that the oldest son could say...

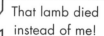

That lamb died instead of me!

PRAY

The Passover happened **just as God had said**. And the Israelites were kept safe **just as God had said**. Thank God that His words always come true.

DAY 60 THE LAMB OF GOD

Yesterday we saw that the Israelites were to celebrate Passover every year, to remember how God rescued them from Egypt. Jewish people were still celebrating Passover 1300 years later at the time of Jesus, and they still do today.

Did you know?

The very first Easter happened at Passover time. That wasn't by accident! Passover and Easter are both about **Rescue**.

We're going to jump into the New Testament to discover something that John the Baptist said about Jesus.

READ
John 1v29

Fill in the gaps.

There is the **L_____** of **G_____** , who takes away the **S_____** of the world!

John was saying that Jesus is like a Passover lamb!

Like a Passover lamb, Jesus died in our place, as our **Rescuer**. It may seem strange, but Jesus is also our **Judge**. To find out more turn to **Judge and Rescuer** after Day 13.

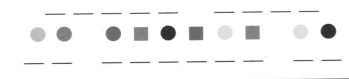

| C = ■ | E = ■ | J = ■ | R = ● | T = ● |
| D = ■ | I = ■ | O = ● | S = ● | U = ● |

If you have put your trust in Jesus, you can say…

Jesus died instead of me!

PRAY
Father God, thank You for sending Jesus to die in my place so that I can be forgiven.

DAY 61

xtb Exodus 12v31-38

What is today's title? *Use yesterday's code to find out.*

Right from the beginning of Exodus we've seen God's promise that He will rescue the Israelites from Egypt. Now, at last, it's time for them to leave.

READ
Exodus 12v31-36

The Israelites had a long journey ahead of them. Circle the things they took with them.

Wow! God had kept His promise. The Israelites were free at last! But God had kept another promise as well...

700 years before, God had promised Abraham that he would have a h-u-g-e family. So enormous that trying to count them would be like trying to count all the stars in the sky! (*This promise is in Genesis 15v5.*)

READ
Exodus 12v37-38

How many men were there? (v37)

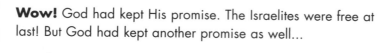

They only counted up the **men**. If you add the women and children there were probably over **Two Million Israelites!!** God really had kept His promise to Abraham!

PRAY **God _always_ keeps His promises. Thank Him that He is like this.**

DAY 62 **FLASHBACK**

FLASHBACK ONE

Yesterday we saw that God had promised Abraham a h-u-g-e family. God also told Abraham what would happen to his family.

READ
Genesis 15v12-14

What did God tell Abraham?
(*Fill in the gaps.*)

punish   great
slaves   country
400

- His family would be strangers in another
  _____ .

- They would be _____ .
- They would be ill-treated for _____ years.
- God would _____ the nation
  who made them slaves.
- They would leave that country with
  _____ wealth.

Did God's words come true? **Yes / No**

FLASHBACK TWO

Joseph was Abraham's great grandson. God used Joseph to save his family from famine in Canaan. Instead they went to live in Egypt. When Joseph was very old, he told his brothers what to do with his body.

READ
Genesis 50v24-26

Joseph believed that God would keep His promise to take the Israelites back to Canaan. **He was right!**

Check out what happened to Joe's body in **Exodus 13v19**

Did Moses take Joseph's body out of Egypt? **Yes / No**

Abraham and Joseph both believed that God's words would always come true. **Do you?**

Yes

If you do, it's because God has helped you to trust Him. Thank Him for helping you to believe.

Not sure

If you're not sure, ask God to help you to believe.

DAY 63 PILLAR CASE

The story so far...

Over two million Israelites have left Egypt, taking gold and silver with them, and also Joseph's body. God has told them to celebrate this rescue every year, and tell their children all about it. (This is in Exodus 12v43-13v16.) But now that the people are free, they have a long journey to make...

When a tourist guide takes visitors through busy streets, he often holds up an umbrella to follow, so they don't get lost. *Follow the umbrellas through the puzzle.*

 Shows where God led the Israelites.

Shows what will happen if they are scared.

Shows the shortest route.

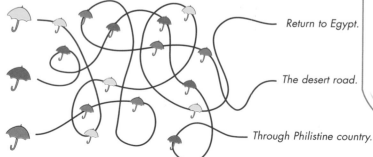

Return to Egypt.

The desert road.

Through Philistine country.

The Israelites didn't follow an umbrella! God gave them something much better.

READ
Exodus 13v17-22

Draw what the Israelites followed.

By day	By night

The Israelites didn't get lost once! God's pillar was always there, guiding them.

PRAY

Psalm 119v105 says, **'Your word is a lamp to guide me, and a light for my path.'** Ask God to guide you as you read His Word, the Bible, and to show you the best way to live for Him.

MAKING A SPLASH

After the Israelites left, Pharaoh changed his mind again.

What have we done?

We've let our slaves go!

So he set off to chase them...

...taking the whole army with him!

They caught up with the Israelites by the Red Sea.

Check out page 13 of your Mini Map Book to see where they were.

The Israelites were terrified!

Why did you bring us here to die?

But Moses trusted God.

Don't be afraid! God will fight for you.

Then God moved the pillar of cloud...

...between the two groups.

You can read this story in Exodus 14v1-14.

For now the Egyptians were cut off. But the Israelites still needed to escape...

READ
Exodus 14v15-22

What did God tell Moses to do? (v16)

Draw what happened.

THINK + PRAY

Imagine what it was like to walk across the bottom of the sea, between two huge walls of water! How would <u>you</u> have felt? What would you think about **God**? Our great God is just the same today. How does that make you feel? Talk to Him about it.

DAY 65 SAFE AT LAST?

The Israelites had escaped across the Red Sea—but the Egyptians were right behind them!

READ
Exodus 14v23-28

What did the Egyptians realise? (v25)

> The **L**_____ is
> **f**_____ against us!

But it was too late! God sent the waters back to their place, and the Egyptian army was trapped.

READ
Exodus 14v29-31

When the Israelites saw God's great power, what did they do? (v31)

They put their trust in **G**_____ and also in **M**_____

All through Exodus we've been asking **"Who is the King?"** What is the answer?   **G**_____ is the true King.

But there's another question: **"What must the Israelites do now that they are rescued?"**

*Copy the **red letters** (in order) to discover the answer.*

W _ _ _ _ _ _ _

Check your answer in Exodus 3v12

Exodus keeps telling us *(16 times so far!)* that the Israelites are to worship God. God is their true King, so it is right to praise Him and to obey Him.

Will **they** praise and obey God?

We'll find out in the next part of **Exodus** *(and in Issue Four of XTB).*

Will **you** praise and obey God?

Will you **praise** God for being your true King? Do you want to **obey** Him in every part of your life? If you do, then ask Him to help you.

TIME FOR MORE?

Have you read all 65 days of XTB?
Well done if you have!

How often do you use XTB?
- Every day?
- Nearly every day? ✓
- Two or three times a week?
- Now and then?

XTB comes out every three months. If you've been using it every day, or nearly every day, that's great! You may still have a few weeks to wait before you get the next issue of XTB. But don't worry!—that's what the extra readings are for...

XTB TIME

When do <u>you</u> read XTB?

at bed time

In the morning.

When I get back from school.

At bedtime.

EXTRA READINGS
The next four pages contain some extra Bible readings from Hebrews chapter 11. If you read one each day, they will take you 26 days. Or you may want to read two or three each day. Or just pick a few to try. Whichever suits you best. There's a cracking wordsearch to solve too...

The extra readings start on the next page

PEOPLE OF FAITH

In the Old Testament there are lots of exciting stories about people who had faith in God. Chapter 11 of Hebrews (in the New Testament) tells us more about their faith.

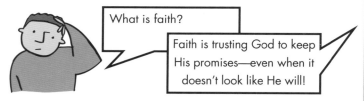

What is faith?

Faith is trusting God to keep His promises—even when it doesn't look like He will!

The ideas in the box will help you as you read Hebrews 11.

PRAY Ask God to help you to understand what you read.

READ Read the Bible verses, and fill in the missing word in the puzzle.

THINK Think about what you have just read. Try to work out one main thing the writer is saying.

PRAY Thank God for what you have learnt about Him.

There are 26 Bible readings on the next three pages. Part of each reading has been printed for you—but with a word missing. Fill in the missing words as you read the verses. Then see if you can find them all in the wordsearch below. Some are written backwards—or diagonally!

If you get stuck, check the answers at the end of Reading 26.

W	O	R	S	H	I	P	P	E	D	R	A	T	S	A
P	L	E	A	S	E	D	R	S	T	A	R	S	B	B
O	W	F	H	O	P	E	A	N	G	E	L	E	T	R
O	A	U	A	B	C	C	I	T	Y	S	L	O	W	A
R	L	S	V	E	I	L	S	H	E	D	I	E	D	H
E	L	E	E	R	A	C	E	A	N	N	O	A	H	A
V	S	D	E	T	S	E	T	P	U	E	N	S	F	M
O	W	N	G	O	D	S	E	P	T	X	S	H	A	M
S	B	A	H	A	R	A	L	E	H	I	O	E	I	Y
S	E	J	A	C	O	B	Y	N	R	S	U	S	T	D
A	A	S	U	S	E	J	R	T	E	T	L	I	H	O
P	R	O	M	I	S	E	D	O	E	S	E	N	O	B

Tick the box when you have read the verses.

1 ☐ **Read Hebrews 11v1-2**

Faith means trusting that God's words in the Bible are true, and that God will keep all His promises.

"Faith is being sure of what we h _ _ _ for." (v1)

2 ☐ **Read Hebrews 11v3**

God created EVERYTHING—just by saying it must be made!

"The universe was created by G _ _ ' _ word." (v3)

3 ☐ **Read Hebrews 11v4**

Cain & Abel were Adam & Eve's sons. Abel had faith in God, and gave Him the best of his flock as a sacrifice. But Cain was angry, and killed his brother.

"By faith A _ _ _ offered God a better sacrifice than Cain did." (v4)

4 ☐ **Read Hebrews 11v5**

Enoch was Adam's great, great, great, great grandson! Genesis 5 tells us that he 'walked with God' for 300 years. Enoch didn't die. God just took him!

"Before Enoch was taken up, he had p _ _ _ _ _ _ God." (v5)

5 ☐ **Read Hebrews 11v6**

The ONLY way to please God is by faith.

"Anyone who comes to God must believe that He e _ _ _ _ _ ." (v6)

6 ☐ **Read Hebrews 11v7**

Imagine being told to build a HUGE boat miles from the sea! Noah had faith—and he built the ark.

"N _ _ _ obeyed God and built an ark to save his family." (v7)

7 ☐ **Read Hebrews 11v8**

God told Abraham to leave his home, his father's family and his country. Abraham trusted and obeyed God.

"By faith A _ _ _ _ _ _ _ obeyed." (v8)

8 ☐ **Read Hebrews 11v9-10**

God made three amazing promises to Abraham, Isaac and Jacob. He promised Land, Children and Blessing. You can find out more about these promises on Day 16 of XTB.

"By faith Abraham lived as a foreigner in the country that God had p _ _ _ _ _ _ _ him." (v9)

9 ☐ **Read Hebrews 11v11-12**

Abraham trusted God to give him a son, even though he and Sarah were now too old. God kept His promise!

"His descendants were as numerous as the s _ _ _ _ in the sky." (v12)

10 ☐ **Read Hebrews 11v13**

Faith means trusting that God will keep His promises. That's what the people in Hebrews 11 believed.

"All these people were still living by faith when they d _ _ _ ." (v13)

11 ☐ **Read Hebrews 11v14-16**

The people in Hebrews 11 were looking forward to being with God in heaven.

"God has prepared a c _ _ _ for them." (v16)

12 ☐ **Read Hebrews 11v17-18**

God tested Abraham by telling him to kill his own son as a sacrifice. Abraham was willing to do it because he loved God more than anything or anyone else.

"By faith Abraham, when God t _ _ _ _ _ him, offered Isaac as a sacrifice." (v17)

13 ☐ **Read Hebrews 11v19**

God provided a ram to die in Isaac's place. In the same way, God provided His own Son Jesus to die in our place, so that we can be forgiven. Three days later, God brought Jesus back to life!.

"Abraham reckoned that God could r _ _ _ _ the dead." (v19)

14 ☐ **Read Hebrews 11v20**

God had made three amazing promises to Abraham. He renewed those promises to Abraham's son Isaac, and his grandson Jacob.

"By faith Isaac blessed J _ _ _ _ and Esau." (v20)

15 ☐ **Read Hebrews 11v21**

By the time Jacob died he was living in Egypt (not the land God had promised!). But Jacob continued to trust God and to worship Him.

"Jacob leaned on his staff and w _ _ _ _ _ _ _ _ _ God."

16 ☐ **Read Hebrews 11v22**

Joseph was sure that God would bring the Israelites back out of Egypt. He told his family to carry his body back to Canaan with them.

"By faith Joseph gave instructions about his b _ _ _ _ _ _ ." (v22)

17 ☐ **Read Hebrews 11v23**

The king of Egypt ordered that all Israelite baby boys were to be drowned. But Moses' parents hid him—and trusted God.

"By faith Moses' parents hid him for t _ _ _ _ months." (v23)

18 ☐ **Read Hebrews 11v24-27**

Moses was brought up by Pharaoh's daughter. But instead of living as an Egyptian, he became the leader of the Israelites and trusted God in the face of suffering.

"By faith Moses r _ _ _ _ _ _ _ to be known as the son of Pharaoh's daughter." (v24)

19 ☐ **Read Hebrews 11v28**

The Passover was the last of the ten plagues. The Israelites sprinkled blood on their doors and trusted God to keep their children safe.

"By faith Moses kept the P _ _ _ _ _ _ _ _ and the sprinkling of blood." (v28)

20 ☐ **Read Hebrews 11v29**

God made a dry path through the Red Sea to rescue the Israelites from the Egyptian army.

"By faith the people crossed the Red Sea as if on d _ _ land." (v29)

21 ☐ **Read Hebrews 11v30**

Joshua led the Israelites into Canaan. Their first battle was for the city of Jericho. God won the battle for them!

"By faith the W _ _ _ _ of Jericho fell." (v30)

22 ☐ **Read Hebrews 11v31**

Rahab lived in Jericho—but she believed that God would give victory to the Israelites, so she helped Joshua's spies.

"It was faith that kept R _ _ _ _ from being killed." (v31)

23 ☐ **Read Hebrews 11v32-38**

These verses list many other people of faith. One is probably Daniel, who trusted and obeyed God, even when faced by hungry lions!

"—they shut the mouths of l _ _ _ _." (v33)

24 ☐ **Read Hebrews 11v39-40**

These people all trusted God—even though they didn't see all of the answers to God's promises.

"These were all commended for their f _ _ _ _." (v39)

25 ☐ **Read Hebrews 12v1**

Having read about so many people of faith, what should we do? Keep going! And keep trusting!

"Let us run with determination the r _ _ _ that lies before us." (v1)

26 ☐ **Read Hebrews 12v2-3**

Think about Jesus—He died for us and rose again. He has done everything for us. So keep on following and trusting Him. Don't give up!

"Let us keep our eyes fixed on J _ _ _ _." (v2)

WHAT NEXT?

XTB comes out every three months.
Each issue contains 65 full XTB pages, plus
26 days of extra readings. By the time
you've used them all, the next issue of XTB
will be available.

ISSUE FOUR: *Travels Unravelled*

Issue Four of XTB finishes the books of Matthew, Exodus and
Acts. It dips into some of Paul's letters as well.

- Investigate the very first Easter in **Matthew's** Gospel.
- Wander through the wilderness with the Israelites in
  Exodus.
- Join Paul as he travels to Rome in **Acts**, and writes to
  some of the people he visited on his journeys.

Available from your local Good Book
Company website:

UK: www.thegoodbook.co.uk

North America: www.the goodbook.com

Australia: www.thegoodbook.com.au

New Zealand: www.thegoodbook.co.nz

Look out for these special seasonal editions of XTB!

Christmas Unpacked

Three weeks of Bible readings to help you focus on
what Christmas is really all about. Meet Dr. Luke
as he tells you all about God's Rescue Plan.
Find out WHO the Rescuer is and WHY we need
rescuing. *Comes with free Rescue stickers.*

Easter Unscrambled

Unscramble the meaning of Easter with the help of
Dr. Luke. Discover what the last part of Luke's book
tells us about Who Jesus is and Why He came.
Comes with free Rescue stickers.

Summer Signposts

A three week Summer Expedition to discover the
real Jesus. Zoom in on the seven signposts from
John's book about Jesus. Follow the clues to
discover Who Jesus is and Why He came. *Comes
with a free magnifying glass.*

Do you know any good jokes?
—send them in and they might appear in XTB!

Do you have any questions?
...about anything you've read in XTB.
—send them in and we'll do our best to answer them.

Write to: XTB, The Good Book Company, Blenheim House, 1 Blenheim Road, Epsom,
Surrey, KT19 9AP, UK **or e-mail me:** alison@thegoodbook.co.uk